A ROOKIE READER®

ADDITION ANNIE

By David Gisler

Illustrated by Tom Dunnington

Prepared under the direction of Robert Hillerich, Ph.D.

CHILDRENS PRESS®

CHICAGO

Library of Congress Cataloging-in-Publication Data

Gisler, David.
    Addition Annie / by David Gisler ; illustrated by Tom
Dunnington.
       p. cm. — (A Rookie reader)
    Summary: Addition Annie counts everything around
her, from trees and knees to little peas.
    ISBN 0-516-02007-2
    [1. Counting—Fiction. 2. Stories in rhyme.]
I. Dunnington, Tom, ill. II. Title. III. Series.
PZ8.3.G4246Ad   1991
[E]—dc20   91-17654
                                             CIP
                                              AC

This is Annie.

4

She adds things up.

1 and 1 are 2.

8

Annie knows that's true.

2 and 1 are 3.

She counts everything—

2+2=4

trees,

2+3=5

peas,

3+3=6

and many knees.

4+2 = 6

18

Addition Annie always adds.

She wants to know how many.

5+2=7

4+3=7

22

She counts everything—

4 + 4 = 8

buttons,

5+4=9

bows,

and her little fat toes.

6+4 = 10

Addition Annie always
knows how many.

WORD LIST

addition	counts	knows	to
adds	everything	little	toes
always	fat	many	trees
and	her	peas	true
Annie	how	she	up
are	is	that's	wants
buttons	knees	things	
bows	know	this	

About the Author

David Gisler is in fifth grade. He has two older sisters, Tricia and Ann, and an older brother, Mark. David has been around authors all his life. His mother has a syndicated education column and has written fifty-five books, including a Rookie Reader entitled *Pancakes, Crackers, and Pizza*. Math is David's favorite subject in school. He also enjoys playing soccer, tennis, and basketball. David is already hard at work on a second book.

About the Artist

Tom Dunnington hails from the Midwest, having lived in Minnesota, Iowa, Illinois, and Indiana. He attended the John Herron Institute of Art in Indianapolis and the American Academy of Art and the Chicago Art Institute in Chicago. He has been an art instructor and illustrator for many years. In addition to illustrating books, Mr. Dunnington is working on a series of paintings of endangered birds (produced as limited edition prints). His current residence is in Oak Park, Illinois, where he works as a free-lance illustrator and is active in church and community youth work.